The Story of
CELTIC

The Story of
CELTIC

JAMES McIVOR *and* MICHAEL MARTIN

BENCHMARK BOOKS
passing on the passion

Celtic are one of the biggest football clubs in the whole world.

The team play their home matches in a huge stadium in front of 60,000 supporters and their players are looked up to as heroes.

They have won all the Scottish competitions many times and, back in 1967, they even lifted the greatest trophy of them all – the European Cup.

But Celtic were not always so famous and successful: the club began life as a way of raising money to feed poor, hungry people in Glasgow…

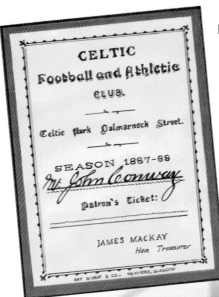

CELTIC
Football and Athletic
CLUB.

Celtic Park Dalmarnock Street.

SEASON 1887-88
Mr John Conway

Patron's Ticket:

JAMES MACKAY
Hon Treasurer

Near the end of the 19th century – over 100 years ago – many people in Glasgow were so poor they could not even afford to buy food.

Some had come to Scotland from Ireland, where a terrible famine had killed hundreds of thousands of people.

They came in search of a better life but times were hard in Scotland, too. Many Scottish people were suspicious of the Irish, who spoke differently and who had a different religion.

In the East End of Glasgow, there was a Marist brother called Walfrid, who worked among the poor people.

Brother Walfrid was worried that so many of his people were going hungry. One day he had a brilliant idea. He would start up a football club, people would pay to see the matches, and he could use the money to buy food.

The only problem was finding a name for the new team. Again, Brother Walfrid had a brainwave.

He decided to call it Celtic – a word that can be used to describe both Scottish and Irish people.

On May 28, 1888, Celtic played their first game, against another team from Glasgow.

The other team was called Rangers and Celtic won the match 5–2. It was the first ever Old Firm match.

OLD FIRM

Celtic and Rangers have been known as the 'Old Firm' for more than 100 years. People realised that the clubs were making lots of money from their fans' rivalry. Whenever they played each other huge crowds would pay to watch – so despite being 'enemies' they were also business partners. Newspaper cartoon strips would show club bosses carrying big bags of money to the bank after a match. The Old Firm derby is one of the most famous games in the world.

Celtic's first stadium was built next to a cemetery but the club soon moved to a new ground.

Fans said it was like going from the graveyard to Paradise. Even now, supporters still refer to Celtic Park as *Paradise*.

Willie Maley was the first manager and
he would remain in charge for
43 years. Willie Maley
brought many great players
to Celtic – men such as
Jimmy Quinn,
Patsy Gallacher
and Jimmy McGrory.

Jimmy McGrory was a human goal machine: he scored 550 times for Celtic in 15 years.

In league football, he scored 410 goals in 408 games. That works out at more than a goal in every match – but in one game he hit the back of the net *eight* times!

HOOPS

Celtic's green and white hooped strip is famous all over the world. But their first shirt was plain white with a shamrock on it, and then they switched to green and white vertical stripes. In 1903 they changed to the Hoops and it became the Celtic strip. Fans roar the team on by shouting, 'Come on the Hoops!', and the chant can often be heard ringing around Celtic Park.

Celtic enjoyed many happy days under Willie Maley, but they also had one of their saddest.

During an Old Firm match on September 5, 1931, Celtic's young goalkeeper, John Thomson, dived bravely at the feet of Rangers striker Sam English.

Sam's knee accidentally struck John's head, and everyone knew something was wrong when he did not get back to his feet.

John was rushed off to hospital, but it was too late to save him and he died later that night.

He was only 22 years old. John was buried the following Monday, and 30,000 people lined the streets of Cardenden in Fife to say goodbye to the best goalkeeper in Scotland. Many fans still visit his grave to this day.

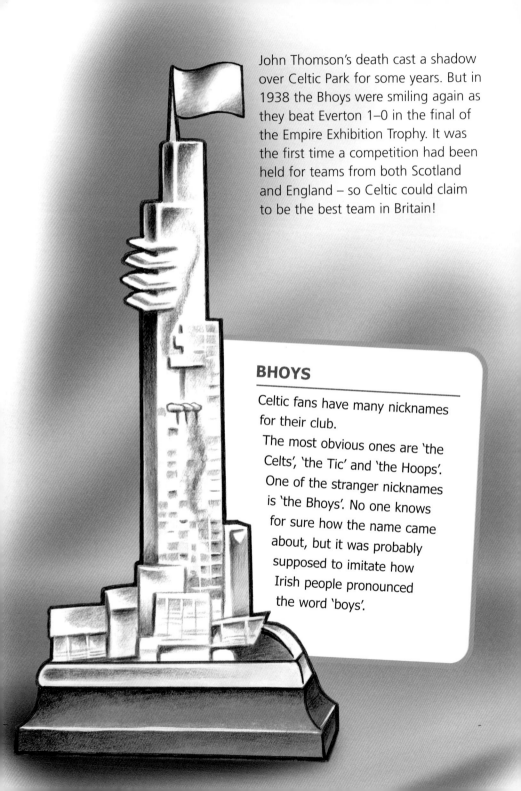

John Thomson's death cast a shadow over Celtic Park for some years. But in 1938 the Bhoys were smiling again as they beat Everton 1–0 in the final of the Empire Exhibition Trophy. It was the first time a competition had been held for teams from both Scotland and England – so Celtic could claim to be the best team in Britain!

BHOYS

Celtic fans have many nicknames for their club.

The most obvious ones are 'the Celts', 'the Tic' and 'the Hoops'. One of the stranger nicknames is 'the Bhoys'. No one knows for sure how the name came about, but it was probably supposed to imitate how Irish people pronounced the word 'boys'.

Jimmy McGrory's goals had not been forgotten at Celtic, and he became manager in 1945.

During Jimmy's time in charge, Rangers were still the strongest force in Scottish football, and Celtic's successes were few and far between. However two of the Hoops' triumphs from that time went down in history.

In 1953 they won the Coronation Cup, held to celebrate Queen Elizabeth II coming to the throne. Like the Empire Exhibition Trophy, the Coronation Cup featured the best teams in England and Scotland so by winning it Celtic could once again say they were the best team in Britain.

An even more famous victory came along four years later …

In 1957 the Old Firm met in the League Cup final and everyone expected Rangers to win. But, amazingly, Celtic not only beat Rangers but thrashed them 7–1! Billy McPhail grabbed a hat-trick, Neil Mochan netted twice, and Sammy Wilson and Willie Fernie also scored as the Bhoys ran riot.

Eight years later there was a new manager in Paradise. His name was Jock Stein and he changed Celtic forever.

'Big Jock' was a tough character, who had worked in the coal mines before becoming a footballer. He made his players work hard but he was also very clever.

By season 1966–67, Jock's team were so good that they won every single competition they entered: the Glasgow Cup, the League Cup, the league championship and the Scottish Cup.

And on May 25 in Lisbon, Celtic were crowned champions of Europe…

In the final of the European Cup, the Bhoys faced a famous team from Italy – Inter Milan – who never imagined they could lose to a team from a small country like Scotland.

But as the two teams lined up in the tunnel, the Inter players began to realise that Celtic did not fear anyone. In fact, much to the astonishment of the Italians, the Scotsmen even had a sing-song as they prepared to take the field.

Bertie Auld started up the chant of *Hail, Hail the Celts are Here*, and the rest of the players joined in, stamping their feet and banging the walls. And the whole of Europe soon realised that Celtic were indeed 'a grand old team to play for'.

Even though Inter were leading 1–0 at half-time, Celtic kept attacking, and eventually broke through the Italian defence – one of the best in the world.

Tommy Gemmell made it 1–1 with a rocket shot, before Stevie Chalmers scored the winner with just five minutes to go.

That team became known as the Lisbon Lions – the best Celtic team ever.

LISBON LIONS

The great Celtic team that won the European Cup in 1967 are known as the Lisbon Lions. The name comes from the city where the final was held – Lisbon in Portugal – and from the courage of the Celtic players, who came from behind to win the match.

The Lions are remembered in many different ways by Celtic fans and, like their manager Jock Stein, they have a stand named after them at Celtic Park.

Nowadays the top teams spend millions on players from all over the world. And recently Celtic have signed players from as far away as Japan and Poland. But, incredibly, Jock Stein's Bhoys were all born within 30 miles of Parkhead!

The Lisbon Lions are: Ronnie Simpson, Jim Craig, Tommy Gemmell, Bobby Murdoch, Billy McNeill, John Clark, Jimmy Johnstone, Willie Wallace, Stevie Chalmers, Bertie Auld and Bobby Lennox.

But that was not all from Jock Stein and his Bhoys. Thanks to great players like Billy McNeill, Jimmy Johnstone, Bertie Auld and Bobby Murdoch, they went on to win the league again, and again, and again, and again… in fact they won the trophy *nine* years in a row.

They also got to the final of the European Cup for a second time but lost 2–1 to Feyenoord from Holland.

Playing for Feyenoord that night was a man called Wim Jansen. Celtic fans would have a lot to thank him for many years later.

Big Jock knew that the Lisbon Lions could not go on forever, so he brought through another batch of brilliant young players to follow in their footsteps. The new generation became known as the Quality Street Kids, and included famous names like Kenny Dalglish, Danny McGrain, Lou Macari and Davie Hay.

Jock retired as manager in 1978, but he will never be forgotten at Celtic Park, especially now that part of the stadium, the Jock Stein Stand, is named after him.

The man who took over from Jock was Billy McNeill, who had lifted the European Cup as captain 11 years earlier. Big Billy led his team to a dramatic league championship win in his first season. Despite losing a man when Johnny Doyle was sent off, Celtic beat Rangers 4–2 in the final match to clinch the title.

Davie Hay, one of the Quality Street Kids, took over from Billy in 1983. Davie's greatest achievement was winning the league in 1986. Hearts had been on top for most of the season, and were two points clear going in to the last match. Celtic had to beat St Mirren by at least three goals, and hope that Dundee could defeat Hearts. Incredibly, the miracle happened – Hearts lost 2–0 and Celtic won 5–0 to lift their 34th championship.

Celtic celebrated their 100th birthday in 1988. Billy McNeill had come back to manage the team again, and his players gave supporters the best present of all when they won the league and cup double.

Rangers had spent millions of pounds on players as they tried to be the best in Scotland, but with players like Paul McStay, Tommy Burns and Frank McAvennie wearing the Hoops they were no match for Celtic in their centenary year.

But the good times did not last …

THE HUDDLE

Along with their star players and noisy fans, Celtic have a secret weapon that helps them win matches. Before kick-off the players put their arms round each other and gather together in the famous Celtic Huddle. Meanwhile, the fans cheer as loudly as they can, and let out a huge roar when the Huddle ends.

It all started in 1995 when Celtic were going through some hard times. One of the players, Tony Mowbray, wanted to find a way of bringing the team closer together – and came up with the Huddle. Tony's team-mates thought his idea was silly at first, but it soon came to be part of Celtic tradition (even though it has been copied by other teams). But the Huddle is still a secret weapon, because the players never reveal what they say when they put their heads together.

Celtic were founded to feed the Glasgow poor but more than 100 years later it was Celtic who were now poor.

Celtic owed the bank millions of pounds but could not pay it back, and the fans were completely fed up with the people in charge. The club was nine minutes away from being shut down forever, but help arrived just in time.

Fergus McCann was a rich businessman who lived in Canada but had grown up supporting Celtic in Scotland. He bought the club, paid the bank and helped Celtic build one of the best stadiums in Europe.

Things soon got better on the park, too…

Tommy Burns returned as manager and led the Bhoys to Scottish Cup glory in 1995 – the first trophy at Celtic Park in six long years. Two years later Wim Jansen – who had played against Celtic in that European final 27 years before – took over as manager. He signed a Swedish striker with dreadlocks called Henrik Larsson.

Back in Jock Stein's day Celtic had won nine league titles in a row and no one thought that record could ever be beaten.

But by 1997 Rangers had equalled it and were desperate to get ten in a row the following season. The Bhoys had to win their last league game to stop them and Henrik Larsson did not let them down.

He scored the first goal as Celtic beat St Johnstone 2–0 to bring the league trophy back to Paradise for the first time in a decade.

Wim Jansen went back home to Holland just two days later but Henrik stayed and scored lots more goals. Even Henrik could not prevent Rangers getting back on top. But that would soon change.

Martin O'Neill took over as manager and told the fans: 'I will do everything I can to bring some success to the football club.'

Martin was as good as his word. The Bhoys beat Rangers 6–2 in his first Old Firm game in charge, and Celtic went on to win the treble. It was the first time for 32 years that they had won the league, League Cup and Scottish Cup in the same season.

Celtic were now the top team in Scotland. But the fans also wanted them to become one of the best in Europe again.

In season 2002–03, they knocked out big teams from England, Spain, Germany and Portugal to reach the UEFA Cup final in Seville.

Celtic fans travelled from all over the world for the club's biggest match in 33 years.

The people of Seville could hardly believe their eyes as more and more supporters poured into their town.

In the end 80,000 were there to cheer on the Bhoys in green and white. They had a wonderful fiesta even though the team lost 3–2 to Porto.

Martin O'Neill's men shrugged off the disappointment of Seville by winning the league and Scottish Cup double the following year.

Hopes were high that 2004–05 would bring even more success, and the Hoops led the championship race for most of the season.

However, the season was to end in sadness. Rangers won the league on the very last day, and then Martin announced that he would have to leave Celtic to care for his sick wife. Martin's last game in charge was the Cup final at Hampden.

Celtic beat Dundee United to lift their 33rd Scottish Cup, but the day will always be remembered for Martin's tearful goodbye to the Celtic supporters.

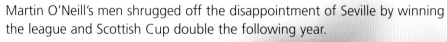

The fans would never forget Martin O'Neill – but Celtic had to look to the future.

They brought in a new manager, Gordon Strachan. He had a disastrous start, losing 5–0 to Artmedia Bratislava in his first game, but managed to turn things around and win the league.

It was Celtic's 40th title, and they won it in record time – with six games still to go.

The next season Gordon's team did even better. Not only did they win the league once again, they lifted the Scottish Cup too. And they had a wonderful adventure in Europe – reaching the last 16 of the Champions League for the first time ever.

But the fun did not end there. In season 2007/08 the race for the league title went to the final day for the third time in five years – but this time Celtic ended up as winners.

Gordon became the first Celtic manager since Jock Stein to win three championships in a row on an unforgettable night at Tannadice as the Hoops beat Dundee United 1-0.

The famous win came just a few days after Celtic coach Tommy Burns died from cancer aged just 51. The supporters were both happy and sad and chanted Tommy's name all night long.

After one more season at the club, Gordon decided to move on. He was replaced by Tony Mowbray, but Tony had a terrible time in charge and left the club after just seven months.

Another former Celt, Neil Lennon, took over. As a player, Neil won eight trophies with the Hoops and he won another one in his first full season as manager. Celtic beat Motherwell 3-0 at Hampden Park to lift the Scottish Cup for the 35th time.

BENCHMARK BOOKS
passing on the passion

The Story of Billy McNeill
The Story of Celtic
The Story of Liverpool
The Story of Manchester United
The Story of Rangers
The Story of the Scotland National Team
The Story of Scotland's Greatest Team

Benchmark Books Ltd
6 Gleneagles Gate, Glasgow G77 5UN

© 2012 Benchmark Books Ltd

ISBN 978 0 9554950 7 6

Illustrated by Doreen Shaw (www.theillustrator.co.uk)
and Alasdair Smith (www.andersonsmithcreative.com)

Printed by Oriental Press, U.A.E.